QUALITY FOR STARTERS

*Guidance for the first steps
in the quality field*

Luis Enrique Diaz

CONTENT TABLE

Preface 1
Introduction 2
What is Quality? 3
1st Goal: They are valuable 5
2nd Goal: Can be trusted 11
3rd Goal: Provide certainty 19
4th Goal: Change to improve 27
Quality Management Systems 33
Six Sigma 53
Lean Manufacturing 71
The next step 88

PREFACE

Quality Engineering is a work field dedicated to generating satisfaction by delivering higher benefits to clients, employees and organizations (public and private). Quality even has an impact in the society, because it enforces the trust between the people. Everybody enjoys quality; the people who receive quality goods and services feel satisfaction; also the ones who work to deliver quality goods and services feel proud of their contribution.

This book contains basic knowledge about quality and will share useful tools to apply and understand it. The content of this book is intended to clarify concepts, apply ideas and take the first steps in this field. Quality is a field that prizes work and effort with benefits and satisfaction.

Be welcome to Quality; I'm convinced that we need more people joining in this field and taking action to improve the benefits that everyone receives as clients, workers or business owners.

INTRODUCTION

This book highlights four basic goals to understand quality purposes and implement it in the organizations. Each element includes a simple tool; this provides a practical reference about the actions that can be taken to apply the ideas in real life.

The content of this book also introduces to 3 work frames, which have been widely used to improve the quality of the organizations. These work frames are too broad to cover them in full detail in this text; however, their purpose and benefits are explained. Every work frame is including a simple tool; this illustrates their application in the organizations.

WHAT IS QUALITY?

Quality is the compound of characteristics that belong to a specific good or service; such characteristics can meet expectations. The recipients of goods and services are the ones who asses the fulfillment of their expectations.

Quality has an impact on people satisfaction and the organization's success. All the clients are looking for goods and services capable of satisfying their expectations. Because of this, people and organizations can establish successful business relationships by exchanging goods and services that fulfill their clients' expectations.

The goods and services that accomplish to deliver high quality are capable of achieving four main goals:
- They are valuable
- Can be trusted
- Provide certainty
- Change to improve

Before covering the details of the four listed elements, is necessary to share three concepts that are common in the quality field. These concepts are frequent in this text:

Products – These are the results generated as a consequence of the organization operations. The products may have different characteristics; they depend on the organization purpose. The term "product" covers goods and services, some examples of products are hardware, assets, information, healthcare, financial, education, communications, food, entertainment and software.

Clients – They are the main recipients of the organization products. The clients have expectations about the products offered to them; they also judge the received products. The actual capability of the products to fulfill the client expectations will define the achieved quality.

Process – These are formulas that establish the way to perform operations within the organization. The processes must operate constantly and help to reach consistent results. A process represents a transformation that takes certain elements (inputs) and produces different ones (outputs). The inputs of the processes have an impact on their results, because of this their characteristics must be controlled; some examples of inputs are raw material, instructions, requests, partially finished goods and resources. The characteristics of the process outputs must match to the expectations; this provides successful results; some examples of outputs are finished goods, information, partially finished goods, defective goods and wastes.

1ST GOAL: THEY ARE VALUABLE

The high-quality goods and services are valuable; this means they have features that allow them to meet the expectations of customers and users. The path to delivering such value includes different stages:

- In the first stage, the expectations of customers must be identified. For this point is required to establish communication channels between the organization and the clients. This way the clients can inform the organization about the features that are important to them.
- In the second stage, the goods and services must be designed considering the clients' expectations. The information obtained in the first stage is the main guide for this purpose, this allows the organization to create products with the proper characteristics. The elements involved in the production of goods and services must fit the expectations established by customers too.
- The third stage is the expectation fulfillment assessment; this stage requires the actual organization outputs. The goods and services produced must be compared to the client's expectations, such expectations are identified as a result of the first stage. This assessment let the organization

know if its results match to the expectations. A complete assessment must consider facts and customer perception.

It is critical to understand that the evaluation just recognizes acceptable results and separates them from the ones that should be corrected. However, there is a chance that evaluation affects interests of members of the organization or third parties; for these cases is needed to take additional measures, to preserve the assessment reliability.

Tool: Checklist

This tool is helpful to verify the value delivered by the organization to its customers. A checklist records the details related to specific facts; such details allow to verify if the products' characteristics match to the ones previously established. Is important to remember the term "product" includes goods and services. The checklist must be easy to use and provide relevant data; this requires a practical and friendly format.

The procedure to develop and use checklists is related to the stages involved in the delivery of valuable goods and services:

1. Establish the product (good or service) to assess; including the specific features that allow the product to meet customers' expectations.
2. Set the proper moment to assess the product; following aspects are relevant and must be considered: feasibility, relevance and required resources.
3. Design the checklist format. The design should allow the registration of the relevant characteristics of the products. The usage of the designed checklist must be easy and practical; simple instructions and graphics resources can be useful for this purpose.
4. Test the checklists. The test is intended to verify that the designed tool serves its purpose. The results of the tests help to identify opportunities to improve its feasibility, relevance and practicality.
5. Record results and actual products characteristics using the checklists. The developed tool should be used to generate

data that shows the real goods and services produced by the organization.
6. Take action when recorded results mismatch the expectations. So the organization handles goods and services which are missing expected results.

Checklist examples:

Checklist: Provided services

Agent's name: _____

Record the daily provided services in this form, select the rows to match the service type.

Date	/ /	/ /	/ /	/ /
Sales				
Unit replacement				
Reimbursement				
Informational				
Other				

```
┌─────────────────────────────────────────────────┐
│              Checklist: Finished units           │
│  Unit Number:_____ Date:___/___/___ Time:__:__│
│  Verified by: _____  │
│  Record the actual characteristics of finished unit. Model: ABC-01│
│                                                  │
│  Mark the proper option:                         │
│  1. The joints present glue residue:  ☐ YES  ☐ NO│
│  2. The joints are fragile:   ☐ YES  ☐ NO        │
│  3. The surfaces are rough:   ☐ YES  ☐ NO        │
│  4. The surfaces are not painted:  ☐ YES  ☐ NO   │
│                                                  │
│  Use the following image to mark the unpainted parts:│
│              [image of furniture frame]          │
└─────────────────────────────────────────────────┘
```

The checklist application provides multiple benefits to the organizations:

- Creates data to know the reality of the company, by recording specific events.
- Demonstrate the delivery of goods and services with valuable characteristics.

- Help to identify conditions that do not match the expectations, which are meant to be solved by the company.
- Generates evidence regarding the verification performed by the organization; this is an effort to know the actual results.

2ᴺᴰ GOAL: CAN BE TRUSTED

Clients trust organizations that provide consistent results; this is based on many delivered goods and services, all of them covering features that meet their expectations. Customers appraise consistent results; they are an essential quality requirement; only high-quality products and services are capable of keeping the expected results through time, earning the trust of the customers. The application of standards to work has a relevant effect to achieve consistency. The organization must meet two points to reach unity in their results:

- Establish standards to work; such standards must be viable and capable of delivering products with the desired characteristics.
- Firmly apply the works standards through time.

Amendments to the work standards are allowed only when the organization is looking to improve their results; it's also important to keep control over any implemented change. The control implies that every change must affect only the intended elements and the organization must retain the capability to reverse any taken action.

In quality engineering, the processes are essential. The process implementation is one of the first steps to establish work standards. A process defines a work unit; each process applies a transformation to add value. All the process added value collaborates to elaborate tangible goods or provide services. Processes require resources, raw materials, information and various supplies to carry out its work. The process required elements are known as "inputs". On the other hand, processes generate products (goods and services), waste and other outcomes as a result of its operation; the elements generated by process are known as "outputs".

Each process maintains relationships with sources and clients. The sources provide the required inputs. The clients are recipients of the produced outputs. The processes interact with others, some interactions are between processes and some other interactions are between processes and external entities. In each relationship a process takes either the role of a supplier (delivering outputs) or customer (receiving inputs). The relations between processes have a significant impact on the results. The adequately handled relations will increase benefits; on the other hand, the wrongly handled relations will cause problems.

The process idea is widespread in organizations. The clarity of this idea helps to understand and control the organization. Each organization is different, because of this its processes, inputs and outputs are unique. The process, inputs and outputs depend on the nature of each organization, the context and the clients' expectations. To set and modify processes is necessary to identify the impact on the fulfillment of the expectations.

Tool: Flowchart

Flowcharts are visual tools. This tool is widely used to establish, communicate and understand the processes. The flowcharts are practical and have a simple format; these characteristics are the key to its high value.

The flowchart identifies the ordered activities that comprise a process. The flowchart may also consider relevant details such as inputs, outputs, decisions to be taken, people playing roles and control.

Processes are defined to achieve consistent results; they establish relevant details; such details should be fulfilled to reach the expected results. Processes apply a transformation, whenever this transformation is executed correctly the resulting products and services increase their value. The process details are intended to assure their correct execution and their valuable results.

The flowchart shows the path that must be followed to apply a process properly and reach its desired result. This tool also helps to perform activities related to study and manage processes: Control the modifications
- Communicate clearly
- Detailed understanding
- Effective implementation
- Fair evaluation

Since the flowchart is a visual tool, it uses symbols to represent the activities of processes graphically. The shapes of the symbols provide information about the contained activity:

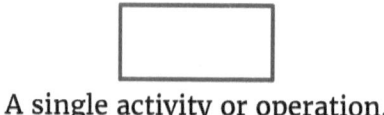

A single activity or operation.

The flow direction from a prior activity to a subsequent one. The tail of the arrow shows the previous activity, the head of the arrow indicates the following activity.

A decision based on a question; Depending on possible answers emerge different flows.

A delay or waiting time.

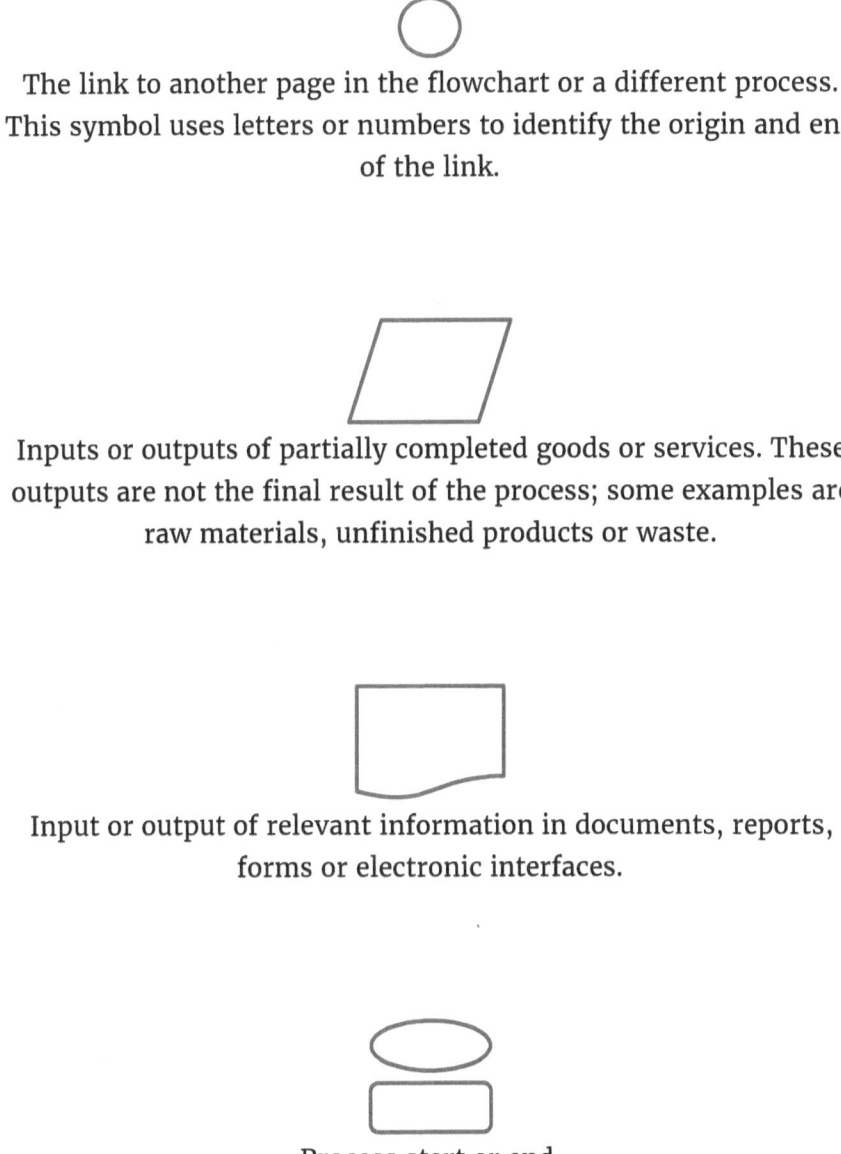

The link to another page in the flowchart or a different process. This symbol uses letters or numbers to identify the origin and end of the link.

Inputs or outputs of partially completed goods or services. These outputs are not the final result of the process; some examples are raw materials, unfinished products or waste.

Input or output of relevant information in documents, reports, forms or electronic interfaces.

Process start or end.

The procedure to draw a flowchart is as follows:

1. Identify the process to draw on the diagram.
2. Define the scope of the process: the starting point, the ending point and the level of detail.
3. Brainstorm the activities carried out in the process. Write the activities in paper pieces or cards; this allows to redistribute them on the workspace and modify them.
4. Sort the activities in the same sequence they are executed in the process, start with the first activity and end with the last one.
5. After establishing the sequence, use arrows to show the process flow. The tail of each arrow indicates a prior activity and the head of the arrow indicates the following activity.

To successfully develop a flowchart is required the participation of the person in charge of the process and those who operate it. Some actors can enrich the flowchart; this is because they interact with the process and provide a broader perspective of it. Some of these actors are customers, suppliers, other areas of the organization. The participation of different people in the flowchart elaboration helps to reach a full understanding of the process and clarify any relevant detail.

The following example shows a manufacturing process flow:

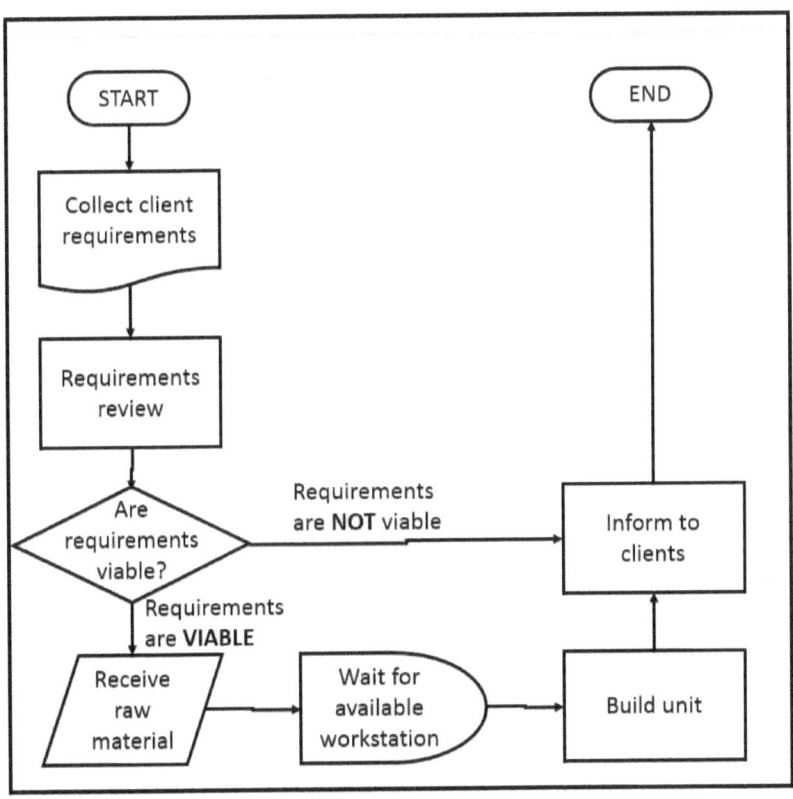

A flowchart can use a wide variety of symbols. Industries standards and reference authors present different symbols and variations. It's important to be aware that not all authors agree on the exact usage or the meaning of the symbols; these different voices must be useful to the organization to choose and take advantage of the different options. At the end the organization must define the rules to build rich and useful flowcharts, aiming to a common understanding of the processes.

To reach common understanding and agreement regarding the processes are the main objectives of the flowchart. Clarity in its content allows to follow the established path, the discipline at its execution will provide consistent results and increase the trust from the clients.

3RD GOAL: PROVIDE CERTAINTY

The knowledge of the reality provides certainty about what happened and any taken action. This knowledge will enable the company to act accordingly to its context, demonstrate the performance and react timely. For quality purposes, organizations and customers need certainty about the following points:

- Developed and delivered products
- The actual operations that originated the products
- The reached compliance regarding the expectations

To provide certainty, the organization should develop mechanisms to identify, record and handle the incidents that affect the results quality. The relevance of the incidents depends on two main factors:

- The effects on the customer's expectations
- The scope of its consequences

Example: an incident that affects the superficial appearance, which has little interest of the customer, will have minimal relevance; on the other hand, an incident that affects the health of the user will have maximum relevance.

The relevant details of products and operations may occur at different moments and points of time; some stages where these details may arise are design, planning, production, implementation, post-sale and customer follow-up.

There are multiple documents and work tools that record incidents which are essential for quality. Some examples are purchase requests, operation reports, invoices, complaints/suggestions, checklists, official communicates and meeting minutes. This information is the basis for certainty.

The Information that provides certainty about the quality is a valuable asset and must generate benefits to the organization; some uses for such information are: demonstrate compliance, solving incidents, develop new knowledge, assess performance and make decisions. The following characteristics are important to use this information: understandable, relevant, timely, close to reality and free of interest conflicts.

The organization can apply statistical tools to the information. These tools will provide new approaches, enrich the study and open the opportunity to more uses.

To provide certainty, the organization must take into account its context and the expectations of the customers; these elements will help to implement the following actions:

- Define the case types that are relevant; such cases should be acknowledged and addressed.
- Establish and execute mechanisms to identify, address and register the actual cases.

- Use the generated data to know the reality of the organization, understand its behavior and act accordingly.

Tool: Box plot

The box plot is a useful tool to analyze the business data; it helps to get a better understanding of the reality and act accordingly. This tool presents a perspective that considers one or more groups of elements; this provides certainty about overall behavior instead of single isolated cases.

Many elements record the relevant information about products (either goods or services). Some items that record such information are purchase requests, operation logs, activity reports, assessments results, checklists, customer satisfaction surveys, delivery notes.

Box plot integrates individual records, applies a few statistical references and generates a visual resource where the behavior of one or more groups can be seen and understood. The Box plots that display information of two or more groups of elements allow comparing their behavior, identifying similarities and differences.

Box plot integrates information regarding the groups' elements and distributes them into four ranges. Each range has mutually exclusive values and an equal count of elements (each range contains 25% of them). The different ranges in the box plot are showing the location of the values close to the center and the ones which are extremely high or low.

The short ranges mean that the contained elements bear a strong likeness between them; on the other hand, the wide ranges mean that the contained elements show significant differences among them or the presence of at least one unusually different element.

Groups that share similar sections in the box plot behave alike; groups allocated at higher sections have bigger values and groups placed at lower sections present smaller values.

This tool draws each group of elements using a box. The boxes have different sections; every section belongs to a range that contains 25% of the group's items. The four sections together congregate 100% of the items in the group:

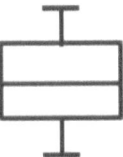

- The bottom line of the box shows the range that contains the elements with the lowest values. This range is holding 25% of the items within the group.
- The rectangle in the center shows the range that holds the elements with middle values; this range contains 50% of the items of the group. The line that divides the rectangle designates the point that separates the group into two halves; a half have values higher than this point and the other has values lower than it.
- The top line of the box indicates the range that contains the elements with the highest values. This range is holding 25% of the items of the group.

Box plot makes easier to compare different groups. This tool is also useful to visualize the changes in the same group over time. Example:

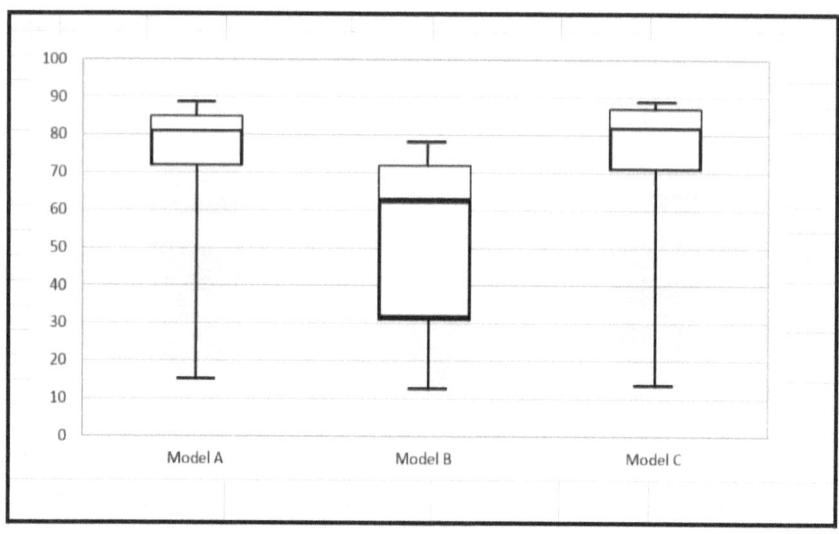

This diagram displays the defective units per day in 3 produced models: A, B and C. The following data belongs to the shown example; this information was calculated using spreadsheets and the daily defects recorded for the models A, B and C:

Groups	Minimum	Percentile 25°	Median	Percentile 75°	Maximum
Model A	16	72	81	85	89
Model B	12	31	63	72	78
Model C	13	71	82	87	89

The diagram displays a lower defect production at model B; this is based on the daily production data. The lower defect production at model B means better performance than the other models (A and C). The diagram also presents the following relevant conditions:

- 50% of the days the models A and C present between 80 and 90 defective units; on the other hand model B never reaches 80 defective units in a single day.
- 25% of the days the models A and C present between 13 and 72 defective units; on the other hand, 50% of the days the model B produces between 12 and 63 defective units. Model B duplicates the best performance at models A and C (Model B with 50% of the days against Models A and C with 25% of the days each).
- 50% of the days model B defects exceed 63 units, models A and C exceed 65 defects in more than 75% of the days.

The following procedure can be used to create a box plot:
1. Define the groups to be displayed.
2. Identify the values of the elements that belong to each group.
3. Sort the items in each group based on their value; start with the lowest until reaching the highest one.
4. Locate the highest value (maximum) and the lowest value (minimum) at each group.
5. Identify in every group the value that is superior to the lowest quarter of its members. This value is known as percentile 25° and can be calculated using Excel by the formula "= PERCENTILE(value range, 0.25)".
6. Locate in every group the value that splits it into two halves. This value is lower than half of the items and higher than the other half. This value is known as median and can be calculated using Excel by the formula "= MEDIAN(value range)".
7. Identify in every group the value that is higher than 75% of its members. This value is known as the percentile 75° and

can be calculated using Excel by the formula "=PERCENTILE(value range, 0.75)".
8. Set the plot area. Use the X axis to assign some individual space for each group; Use the Y axis to show the ranges that hold the values present in the groups.
9. Draw a rectangle for each group; the rectangle must fit the values of the 25th percentile and the 75th percentile.
10. Split each rectangle with a line marking the value of the group's median.
11. Draw a line to connect the maximum value of each group with the top side of the proper rectangle.
12. Draw a line to connect the minimum value of each group with the bottom side of the proper rectangle

Box plot summarizes the information related to several items; this presents an overall perspective in a single image. The data contained in the box plot provides knowledge about the behavior of entire groups and their items. The knowledge of whole groups is useful for different purposes:

- The boxplot demonstrates the behavior of groups that perform according to the expectations.

- The boxplot illustrates the gaps between groups that miss the expectations and the actual goals

- The boxplot makes an objective comparison between groups to identify similarities, differences and changes.

4TH GOAL: CHANGE TO IMPROVE

The customers' needs and the organization's context are permanently changing. Organizations must be aware of these conditions and get adapted to them; this will allow the companies to maintain and improve its capability to meet the expectations and deliver quality.

The organization must be responsive to the situations that arise from different sources and require changes. Customers, business partners and authorities are external sources that present their demands to the organization. The organization staff can identify problems that must be solved and opportunities that could be implemented. Local groups and regional leaders reveal circumstances that must be handled. Therefore the organization should establish mechanisms to acknowledge the different arising needs and resolve them.

Different situations may justify changes within the organization; some are incidents that have already taken place and must be solved accordingly; some others are possibilities that have not happened yet, but their potential consequences are enough to take action in advance.

The situations that justify the organization changes can be related to either negative or positive effects; the transformations on such items impact customer satisfaction and other results. Situations with negative effects on the results require changes to resolve and prevent them; on the other hand, situations with positive effects on the results need actions to promote and take advantage of them.

Communication is a crucial element to accomplish the adaptation of the organization. The communication will provide clarity on the path that the organization must follow to implement a change:

- Communication begins by helping to clarify the situation that requires a change in the organization.
- Communication helps to follow the actions that must be executed to transform the organization.
- Communication supports the results assessment, reporting the actual outcomes of the implemented change.

The adaptation of the organization requires the participation of different actors who contribute with skills, perspectives and resolutions; these contributions will assure a successful transformation. The number of involved participants accords to the size and complexity of the change to be implemented.

The changes in the organization require guidance and support from several members of the organization with enough responsibility and authority. The effects of implemented actions and the feasibility of pending tasks are aspects that must be continuously assessed. All these elements will be useful to adjust the scope of the changes and their assigned resources.

Tool: Plan – Do – Check – Act Cycle

The changes that the organization implements require working with clear objectives; as well as a follow-up which try to move to a successful conclusion.

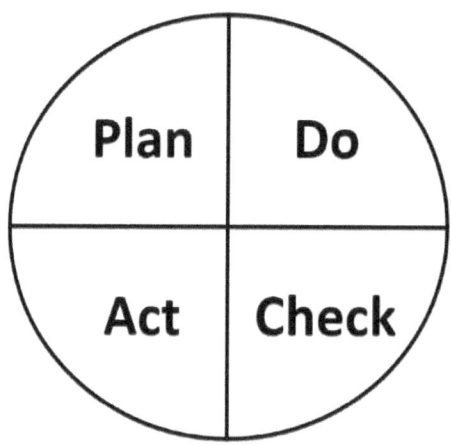

The Plan-Do-Check-Act Cycle is a tool that establishes clear phases to develop changes within the organization; each one of these phases allows to work on specific goals and orderly progress in the implementation of changes. These changes will help maintain and improve the organization's ability to meet expectations.

Plan - This is the first phase of the cycle. Plan stage should reach an agreement regarding the actions that will be executed to implement change; these actions must include specific dates for its conclusion. The organization must try to identify the root causes of the situation that aims to change; these causes are a relevant element to define the proper actions to execute. It is essential to have a clear understanding of the faced problem; facts and objective references will allow the company to know the problem extent and judge the results of the changes.

Do - This is the second phase of the cycle. At Do stage the previously planned actions are executed. It is critical to follow the implementation of planned actions; this aims to avoid omissions. It is also needed to watch the progress in the changes and resolve any incidents which alter the original plans; this is caused by knowledge and cases that arise during the implementation. This stage generates information that enriches the understanding of the company context and the implemented transformation.

Check - This is the third phase. In Check stage the new results are compared against the ones obtained before the implemented actions. The comparison must be conducted carefully to be fair, the context before and after the changes is important to perform a proper evaluation; the knowledge generated during the Do stage is a relevant element for this purpose. The comparison performed at this stage must be based on facts, avoiding any bias and conflicts of interest.

Act - This is the fourth phase. This stage defines the direction of a new course originated from the conclusions reached in the Check phase. If the results generated by the implemented change match the expectations, the organization must close to the transformation process and set measures to ensure its continuity. If the results aren't enough, then is needed to look for new alternatives following the same path: plan-do-check-Act.

Finding solutions to the problems faced by the organization is not as fast as desired; sometimes the deployed actions do not reach the expected results; in some other cases, the outcomes exceed the goals. The Plan-Do-Check-Act Cycle can become part of the organization's permanent pursuit of quality; the very same cycle can support a single execution project. Example:

A furniture factory produces a bookshelf, 1 of every five completed units presents scratches on its surface. Such defects have increased the expenses in the paint at the production line; this increase represents a 20% higher cost than budgeted. The defects in produced units have caused complaints from customers and the company had to reimburse or replace the units returned by the customer.

PLAN - The production line staff dedicated time to analyze the problem; after discussing the causes, the organization members agreed to implement a specific action: protect the painted units. The painted units will be protected using plastic wrap (0.2 in thick); the cover will be applied just after the painted units dry off. Painting workspace and procedure will be modified to include the wrapping tasks; these modifications will be implemented during January first three weeks.

DO - The organization provided wrapping training during January first two weeks; all the painting staff was part of such training. Bookshelf production line was modified during January third week, this update added space for wrapping units. The wrapping supplies were not delivered on time by the provider; this extends the action implementation until January fourth week of January.

CHECK - Every produced bookshelf was assessed during February; this evaluation is focused on the paint. In the first week of the month, 5 of 98 units produced had paint defects, at the second week 7 of 102 bookshelves presented issues, during the third week 6 of 97 had painting flaws, the last week 6 of 100 units included paint defects. The percentage of defective units (per week) ranged between 5% and 7%, consolidating the monthly data the outcome is 6%. The new result is lower than the original one (6%<20%).

ACT – The persistence of 6% defective units justifies additional actions for improvement. The team will work together during March and plan new actions to reduce the painting defects; the new actions are expected to be implemented during May and June.

QUALITY MANAGEMENT SYSTEMS

The quality is affected by multiple elements; such elements interact between them and have the potential to increase benefits or expand problems. The organization can make efforts to handle these elements and earn better results:

- Fulfill client requirements and deliver higher value.
- Produce consistent results to earn customers' trust.
- Generate information that provides certainty Implement transformation to cover the changing needs.

The organizations develop their Quality Management Systems to maximize the benefits and reduce the losses; this is a framework to keep the best possible performance, considering all the quality relevant elements and their interaction.

The Quality Management Systems establishes an agreement regarding the outcomes that the organization must generate and deliver; all the needed contributions from various components are handled to reach this agreement.

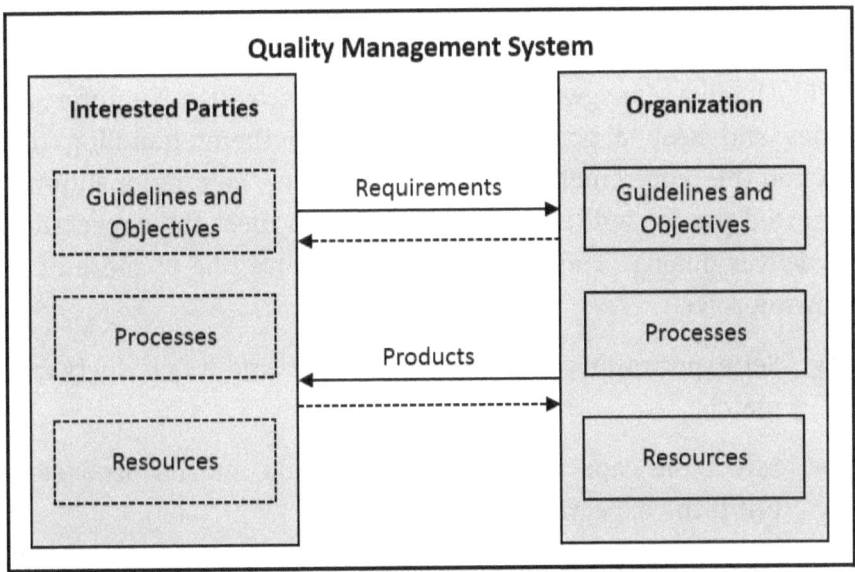

Interested parties

External people, entities and groups that have an impact on the quality of the outcomes generated by the organization. Clients are interested parties; they set several parameters and requirements for quality, if the organization meets such expectations it has successful results. Many organization outcomes are intended to satisfy clients; they will judge the organization quality based on the received products.

Providers are interested parties; they provide elements that are incorporated into the organization operations; the providers' contributions may affect the organization's capability to comply with the quality.

The governments and authorities are interested parties; they establish mandatory requirements for the organization and its products. The authorities will judge the fulfillment of their requirements and penalize non-compliance.

The Quality Management System must recognize the interested parties and keep a good relationship with them, handling their effect on the requirements and its fulfillment. The relationship with interested parties will allow the company to meet the expectations and deliver quality. The interested parties have one or more of the following roles:

- Set expectations that the organization and its products must match.
- Affect the capacity of the organization and its products to fulfill the expectations.
- Judge the organization and its products and determine if the expectations were covered or not.
- They react when the organization and its products do not meet expectations.

Requirements

Specific characteristics and conditions that must be covered by the organization and its results. The value of the organization and its products is affected by the requirement fulfillment; the requirement fulfillment also affects the interested parties judgment. In the most common scenario the requirements are defined by clients and the organization fulfills them with its operations and outcomes; however, there may be other scenarios where the requirements are determined by different actors (authorities, external auditors, internal clients) and other entities assume the responsibility to cover them (suppliers, business partners).

The Quality Management System should enable the organization to perform the following requirement related actions:

- Identify the requirements to cover.
- Follow up the contributions to meet the requirements and control them.
- Use reliable information to assess the requirements fulfillment; considering the context, objective facts, clients' perception and relevant actors feedback.

Quality objectives and guidelines

Different members from the organization must contribute the expected results in terms of quality; these members belong to different parts of the company structure.

All the contributions help the company to accomplish quality and they need support to be successful. There are two elements to provide support to the contributions: Objectives and Guidelines.

- Objectives set specific goals to reach
- Guidelines provide references to execute the operations properly.

Members of the organization at different levels may establish Objectives and Guidelines. The upper levels establish a quality policy (guideline) or the long-term organization's objectives. The lower levels define a protocol for simple operations (guideline) or the daily individual production target.

The Quality Management System must help the organization to perform the following actions:

- Define proper guidelines and objectives to help the different members of the organization

- Identify the guidelines and objectives that belong to each organization member.

- Check the guidelines application and the objectives accomplishment.

Processes

The processes are transformations that must be performed in order to generate valuable products (goods and services). The process set the path to follow and reach the expected results; they represent a steady work formula that provides consistent outcomes. Processes establish a base to understand and control of the organization operation and performance. The Quality Management System focuses on processes that affect the expectations fulfillment.

The most frequent scenario covers processes fully executed within the same organization; although there are some other scenarios where processes are performed outside the company (partially or entirely). The processes executed outside the organization involve external actors as providers and business partners. The Quality Management System must include all the critical processes for customer satisfaction and expectation fulfillment; either if the execution is completed within the organization or if external actors are involved.

The processes commonly establish relationships between them; this means the outputs from a process become the inputs for another one. The relations between processes require attention to ensure their interaction adds value to products and avoid to propagate any damage.

The Quality Management System should enable the organization to perform following activities:

- Set up, understand and apply processes.
- Fairly assess the processes' results.
- Timely monitor processes' progress
- Keep and promote beneficial interaction between processes

Resources

The resources are various elements used by the organization to perform their activities; some of these components have the potential to affect the quality of the organization's results and products. Relevant resources depend on each organization and its purpose and must be appropriately handled. Some resources are personnel, facilities, raw materials, tools, documents, IT infrastructure, software, vehicles, patents.

The resources that affect quality must be capable of providing the expected value; this capability could be based on their characteristics or interactions.

Relevant resources could be found in a variety of scenarios and conditions; such factors must be considered to produce the highest benefits for the organization. The following examples could be considered:

- Resources supplied by providers
- Assets developed by the own organization
- Client's property loaned to the company
- Highly fragile items
- Long lifetime properties
- Devices which require frequent maintenance

Quality Management System must provide the organization the following capabilities:

- Identify and establish the needed resources to deliver the expected products and results.
- Control the resources status to guarantee their contribution.
- To assess the performance and proper use of resources.

Products

Products are the main result of the work performed by the organization; the products include goods and services delivered to customers. Products are a crucial reference to build successful processes; since processes operation must deliver suitable products. Products allow the organizations to match expectations and fulfill the requirements established by interested parties. The products are objective elements to assess the organization.

The products have different properties, depending on the organization that generates them; some products are goods and others are services. Usually the products are produced, from beginning to end, inside of the organization; however, there are scenarios where products are produced partially outside the organization, for this cases the participation of suppliers, business partners and other stakeholders is critical.

The customers are the main recipient of the organization's products. However, there are also products destined for other actors, as stakeholders and organization areas.

It's necessary to work at multiple stages to satisfy the expectations of the products; starting with the clear product concept (design), running the activities to develop the product (production) and delivering it to its recipients (distribution). Some actions are included to solve incidents after the product has been delivered (post sales).

The workflow that builds the products and delivers them to the customers should be controlled; this control will deliver only products that meet the expectations. There is a possibility to deliver products which miss the expectations; however, this requires the approval from customers and the proper entities.

The organization must build elements to provide certainty about the path traveled by the products, until its arrival with customers; this certainty is based on information that clarifies details and facts about the products and their development. The purpose of this information is to provide confidence about the suitability of the products. This information also allows the organization to take action on products that were exposed to risks and harmful situations.

The Quality Management System must enable the organization to perform following activities:

- Design, produce and deliver products that match the expected value.
- Troubleshoot cases where products were unable to provide the expected value.
- Provide certainty about the products and their capability to deliver the expected value.

The components of the Quality Management System (interested parties, requirements, objectives, guidelines, processes, resources and products) must meet the following conditions:

Relevance – Each component has an impact on the quality of the organization and its outcomes (including the products). There are relations between the components and the effect of each one can affect the others.

Control - establishes conditions to keep the immediate results of components within the expectations. The control mechanisms can be oriented to individual elements or combinations of them. The organization identifies situations that deviate from expected and performs actions to solve them.

Direction - Components receive the necessary attention to make their contribution in the medium and long-term. Their performance is assessed to fulfill the organization's expectations. Direction should consider aspects of each component, collections and their interactions. The vision for the future must lead the actions, considering the events of the past and the present context.

Improve - The capability to meet the expectations is increased by taking multiple actions. Some actions are focused on a single component and others affect collections of components. Taken actions provide different benefits: correct the unsatisfactory results, strengthen the successful outcomes, prevent risks and take advantage of opportunities.

Valuable interactions – The components interactions are developed to provide the highest possible benefit. This development requires actors who have skills, convictions and perspectives to produce the best synergy.

Supported by evidence – The knowledge about the reality must be part of the management of the components. This knowledge must be strictly based on evidence. This knowledge is crucial for following purposes: control the operations, continuous improvement and valuable interactions.

The Quality Management System is a set of elements dedicated to the fulfillment of expectations:

- Recognizes those who have relevant interaction with the organization (Interested parties)
- Satisfies the expectations (requirements)
- Receives contributions from all members of the organization (objectives and guidelines),
- Keeps a consistent performance (processes)
- Maintains the necessary assets for the proper execution (resources)
- Develops and delivers suitable outcomes (products).

The Quality Management System helps the organization to define its intended results and work to make them true. Each organization develops its own Quality Management System depending on its context; such system must attend all factors and elements that may affect the performance and outcomes.

ISO 9000

The International Organization for Standardization (ISO) has led the constant development of a standard for the Quality Management Systems: ISO 9000. This standard is a reference for all kinds of organizations which seeks to strengthen the quality and its benefits.

The ISO 9000 standard includes specific requirements; these are included in a particular document: ISO 9001. The organizations are voluntarily audited to demonstrate their ISO 9001 fulfillment; after a successful audit the organizations earn a certificate. There are several options for the audits; every choice has its own prestige and cost.

The ISO 9000 standard considers seven principles that must be applied to every Quality Management System:

1. Customer focus. Organizations depend on their customers and must make an effort to keep them satisfied; this will ensure a profitable relationship in the long term with them. The organization must fulfill customer' expectations and needs.
2. Leadership. The highest levels of the organization determine its direction; for this reason, they must be convinced of the value of quality and promote it across the company. The leaders of the organization must include quality among their priorities, involve staff, support their work and follow up the results. The leaders' influence must help the organization to reach the desired quality.

3. Engagement of people. The organization members must contribute to the expected quality. Every member has different responsibilities, but everyone must make the suitable contribution.
4. Process approach. Processes develop conditions that promote successful outcomes. Promote the processes approach in the organizations established bases of knowledge and operation for all its members; these conditions increase the consistency of the results and a coordinated interaction.
5. Improvement. The organization must strive to reach higher levels of performance and better outcomes. Improvement must be a permanent effort; this will increase the benefits for customers, the organization and other interested parties.
6. Evidence-based decision making. The search for real benefits requires work and decisions based on the organization's reality. Is necessary to rely on information that reflects the facts; this information will encourage productive work and objective decisions.
7. Relationship management. External entities (mainly customers, suppliers and business partners) have an impact on the organization's outcomes. This effect must be controlled to reach the best possible results; communication and collaborative work are essential for this purpose.

ISO 9001 requirements became one of the best references to develop the Quality Management System of the organizations. These requirements are in continuous evolution, by the time this book was published the most recent version is 2015 (ISO 9001:2015).

Tool: Requirements matrix

This tool links the requirements with elements that are dedicated to fulfilling them. The requirements matrix has three sections; each one is dedicated to specific data:

- The quality requirements to cover

- The elements dedicated to satisfying the requirements; these elements could be parts of the Quality Management System (interested parties, processes, products, resources, guidelines, objectives).

- The relationship between the requirements and the components responsible for fulfilling them

The matrix keeps these related elements visible; this helps to take action on the components, considering their potential effects on the requirements compliance.

This tool has a simple structure and must be easy to use; it could be elaborated using spreadsheets or any surface that allows to record information in columns, rows and grids.

Requirements

There must be a space dedicated to identify and explain the requirements; the information to understand each requirement must be included in this space. Some useful data could be related to the requirements' level of relevance or its compliance degree.

To identify the requirements, the organization may use different details; some examples are code names, ID numbers or technical names. The purpose of this data is to refer to each requirement without confusion.

Different information items can be included to understand the requirements: definitions, documents, manuals, training material. All of these items must guarantee the same understanding about expectations to cover.

The references to the requirements' relevance allow to recognize the importance degree of each one; this is very helpful when time and resources are limited. The usage of numeric values is helpful on this references; this enables comparisons between higher and lower importance. The relevance of each requirement must take into consideration the extent of their effects; examples:

- A requirement that provides security conditions for life and health has top importance
- A requirement that grants occasional gains or superficial features has lower relevance.

There are external groups that could help to determine the importance of each requirement; some of these groups are customers, authorities, experts, researchers and industry leaders.

The degree of achieved compliance shows the distance between the actual outcomes and the desired results. It is crucial to consider the facts, context and perception of relevant entities (customers, authorities, auditors). For practical purposes, this degree must be expressed using numeric values.

The organization is free to define the data and format that result most useful in this space. Below example shows the requirements space applied to a furniture store; this includes the definition of fields and the recorded required:

- Codename and common name to identify the requirement
- Definition to have a clear understanding regarding the requirement to fulfill
- Priority, this provides a numerical reference of the requirement's importance; in this example, a numeric scale is applied, 0 means the lowest priority and the highest priority is 10.
- Assessment, this is a reference of the achieved compliance degree; uses a numeric scale, 0 means a total failure and 10 represents complete success.

QUALITY FOR STARTERS

Codename	Common name	Definition	Priority	Assessment
R01	Strong product	Joints must be firm; no gaps are allowed. Further documentation is located at...	10	9
R02	Soft surfaces	surfaces must be sanded and painted. Further documentation is located at...	9	9
R03	Accomplish delivery dates	Products must be delivered on the agreed date. Further documentation is located at..	8	5
R04	Delivery service	Requested delivery service must be provided to the agreed location. Further documentation is located at..	5	10

Elements dedicated to requirements fulfillment

This space of the tool contains the components responsible for reaching the requirements; is expected that most of these components are part of the Quality Management System. Each component should include elements that enable following actions:

- Identify them
- Understand their purpose and behavior
- Verify their actual results
- Plan for the future

Some components that could be included in this space are interested parties, processes, products, objectives, guidelines and resources.

Different details can be used to identify the elements: technical names, keycodes, commercial brands. These data must allow referring to each element without confusions

Assorted knowledge assets can be used to understand the elements: documentation, training material, manuals, signed agreements. All these information pieces provide a common understanding about their operation and purpose.

There must be evidence to demonstrate the actual element's results. This information will provide accurate knowledge regarding the performance and enable the organization to take action.

Planning must be executed to develop each element in the long-term. The aimed goals and the actions to perform must be included in the plan. The organization must work permanently on the plans; this helps to keep delivering the expected results.

The organization is free to determine the data and format that results most suitable in the space assigned to the elements. The example below shows the element space applied to a furniture store; the following fields are included:

- Keycode and name to identify each element.
- Definition to reach the same understanding about the element and their behavior. Since the elements require too much information, a reference to additional documentation is added.
- Records of the elements results; this refers to the location of the full performance evidence.
- Plans for future actions; the location of the comprehensive plans are included.

Keycode	Name	Definition	Records	Plan
PROC-01	Manufacturing process	Process dedicated to building units for the customers. Further documentation at location...	Production line logs and reports. These documents are stored at...	Manufacturing Plan; the Directive board reviews this plan. The complete documentation is stored at...
PROC-02	Distribution Process	Process dedicated to delivering the units to the customer's location. Further documentation at location...	Delivery paperwork. These documents are stored at...	Distribution Plan; the Directive board reviews this plan. The complete documentation is stored at...
RES-01	Cutting machines	Devices to cutting pieces. Further documentation at location...	Production line logs and reports. Maintenance reports. These documents are stored at...	Manufacturing Plan and Maintenance Plan; the Directive board reviews these plans. The complete documentation is stored at...
RES-02	Sanding machines	Devices to sanding pieces. Further documentation at location...	Production line logs and reports. Maintenance reports. These documents are stored at...	Manufacturing Plan and Maintenance Plan; the Directive board reviews these plans. The complete documentation is stored at...
RES-03	Paint and varnish	Resources to coat the products, enhance presentation and duration. Further documentation at...	Supplies purchase orders. Production line logs and reports. These documents are stored at...	Manufacturing Plan and Supplying Plan; the Directive board reviews these plans. The complete documentation is stored at...
RES-04	Painting machines	Devices to applying paint and varnish. Further documentation at...	Production line logs and reports. Maintenance reports. These documents are stored at...	Manufacturing Plan and Maintenance Plan; the Directive board reviews these plans. The complete documentation is stored at...
RES-05	Delivery vehicles	Vans to delivering products to customer locations. Further documentation at...	Delivery paperwork and maintenance reports. These documents are stored at...	Distribution Plan and Maintenance Plan; the Directive board reviews these plans. The complete documentation is stored at...
HR-01	Manufacturing Technician	Human resources dedicated to building the products. Further documentation at...	Production line logs and reports. These documents are stored at...	Manufacturing Plan; the Directive board reviews this plan. The complete documentation is stored at...
HR-02	Delivery agents	Human resources dedicated to delivering units to customer's location. Further documentation at...	Delivery paperwork. These documents are stored at...	Distribution Plan; the Directive board reviews this plan. The complete documentation is stored at...

Relations between requirements and elements

This space displays the effects of each element on the requirements. The perspective of the complete relations enables the organization to take action considering the potential effects; this will provide a better reference for decisions and stronger control on their consequences.

The organization is free to select the data and format design in this space dedicated to the relations between requirements and elements. The example below belongs to a furniture store; in this case, the columns are dedicated to requirements and the rows to the elements. The relations are marked in the cells where requirements match the components responsible for their compliance.

	Keycodes	Requirements					
		R01	R02	R03	R04		
Elements dedicated to requirements fulfillment	PROC-01	X	X				
	PROC-02			X	X		
	RES-01	X	X				
	RES-02		X				
	RES-03		X				
	RES-04		X				
	RES-05			X	X		
	HR-01	X	X				
	HR-02			X	X		

SIX SIGMA

Six Sigma (6σ) is a framework that seeks to reduce the production of defective goods and services. Is based on a cycle to make changes in processes and increase their capability to meet expectations. The transformations carried out in Six Sigma must be based on objective facts.

Six Sigma was developed within the Motorola company; it was intended to reduce the costs and negative effects caused by the defective units. The Six Sigma goal is ambitious: to minimize the production of defects. The name "Six Sigma" is based on statistical concepts: the operation of a process can be very reliable and produce only 3.4 defects per every million opportunities.

Six Sigma affirms that the characteristics of goods and services are the result of the processes that produced them; for this reason, the defects are also a consequence of such processes. With this idea Six Sigma proposes to modify processes, so they no longer generate defective outcomes. Six Sigma follows five work stages:

Define
This is the first Six Sigma stage. The total effect of defective outcomes is measured and documented; costs, defective count and expenses volumes are considered for this purpose. The production of defects and their consequences must be presented as a problem. At this stage, the members of the organization communicate and reach a common understanding of the problem. The documentation

of the impact, including economic terms, will help to define priorities and receive the necessary support to change the current situation.

At Define stage the organization must generate a charter to explain the problem and its effects. This document will be presented to leaders and decision-makers to involve them in the transformation.

Measure

The second stage produces information for the following goals:

- Specify the characteristics of satisfactory goods and services (non-defective).

- Understand the actual operation of processes that produce defective goods and services; this includes their results, relationships with other elements and changes through time.

- Identify defective outcomes (goods and services); this must include the actual conditions when defects were produced.

The information generated in this stage must match to the reality and provide details. Matching the reality allows understanding facts, including their context. Details enable to recognize the specific conditions which affect processes and outcomes.

Measuring instruments are the best tools to describe facts; they are loyal to reality and provide details; such resources must be considered to produce the information of this stage.

The output of this stage is trustworthy information; this will be useful to understand the causes of the problems and generate ideas to solve them. Some sources to consolidate this information are operation records, activity reports, samples, assessments, tests results and surveys.

Analyze

This stage is intended to find the causes of the defects, based on the information gathered on the previous step (Measure). At this stage, the conditions that seem to drive to the production of defective goods and services should be highlighted. Following conditions could be related to a possible defect causes:

- The suspected cause precedes the defect; this means the "probable cause" is present before the moment of producing defective goods or services. If "probable cause" arises just after making the failed outcomes, then it can't be considered responsible.

- The cause is common for poor outcomes; this means the "probable cause" must be constantly present in defective goods and services. If a "probable cause" is unusual at defect outcomes, then it does not seem to be liable for defects.

- The variations in the cause affect the occurrence of defects; this means the "probable cause" increases or decreases will be reflected on the defects production. If changes in the "probable cause" does not match to variations in the production of poor goods and services, then the relationship seems inexistent.

Relations between causes and defects production may have a wide variety of behavior; some examples are listed below:

- When "Condition A" is present, "Defect B" also occurs.
- When "Condition A" does not arise, "Defect B" doesn't occur either.
- When "Condition A" increases, "Defect B" also increases.
- When "Condition A" increases, "Defect B" decreases.
- When "Condition A" decreases, "Default B" also decreases.
- When "Condition A" decreases, "Default B" increases.

The work at this stage must be based on information obtained at the 'Measure' step; this will provide objective bases to the identified causes. The product of this stage is a document that includes the following elements:

- "Probable causes" identified in the production of defective goods and services.
- The ideas to modify processes and their outcomes; changing the "probable cause" aiming to reduce the defect production.
- Clear references to the information sources used to identify the "probable cause" of the defects.

Improve

The fourth stage executes actions to modify the processes and their outcomes; the goal is to reduce the production of defective goods and services. "Improve" stage should implement the ideas generated at "Analyze" step; is necessary to verify the implemented ideas effect on the production of defects.

At this stage, it is necessary to consider the following points:

- The actions must be planned and receive follow-up; this ensures adequate progress in the implementation, within the expected time.
- Establish the scope of actions, the resources required and relevant actors; this will guarantee the necessary support for its successful implementation.
- Record the progress in the execution of the actions, including events that limit or aid its implementation; this will provide bases to evaluate the progress, manage support, make appropriate changes and assess the results.

The results of the executed actions should be assessed, based on objective elements; this requires information after their implementation. The new information must be compared to the one consolidated in the stage "Measure". Only the actual decrease of defective goods and services can confirm the success; otherwise, further actions must be executed to accomplish the desired results.

Control

The last stage is dedicated to preserving the decrease in the production of defective goods and services; this requires the implementation of additional actions with simple objectives:

- Prevent transformed processes from step back and lose the acquired benefits. After implementing a change, there is a risk to get it reversed; therefore, it is necessary to establish mechanisms to avoid a push back. Some mechanisms to avoid a step back are the establishment of policies, training, tools replacement and infrastructure upgrade. The goal is to remove any factor that enforces the former process.
- Fix the cases that do not follow the implemented changes. The organization must identify incidents where the new

process is not respected. The organization must react promptly to correct these cases and avoid its recurrence. Some measures to resolve these situations are reviews, evaluations and audits.
- Resolve the increases in the production of defective goods and services. The performance of the processes should be monitored; if there is an increase in the volume of defective products, the organization must react, identify causes and correct them; this will prevent losing the reached progress. Some alternatives to address defects increases are: supervision, monitoring of processes and result reports

The Six Sigma methodology has been very successful in different organizations around the world; the following factors have fostered its success:

- Six Sigma methodology specialists. Some professionals are dedicated to master the theory and develop projects under Six Sigma methodology; this includes a certification known as Six Sigma Black Belt. To be a Black Belt is necessary lead several projects using this framework, generating objective benefits; in addition, must pass a certification exam. The American Society for Quality is one of the most recognized organizations to earn the Black Belt certification.
- Multidisciplinary teams are involved in Six Sigma projects. This gathers professionals proficient in various fields and with relevant roles in the organization, all of them contributing to the projects. The knowledge, experience and resolution of these professionals produce successful transformations in the processes.

- Objective information as the primary reference. Decisions and transformations in the Six Sigma projects are supported on facts; this provides a high degree of certainty in the results. In Six Sigma instruments of measurement and statistics are used to take advantage of the organization's information.

Not all organizations have the resources to implement Six Sigma in its full extent; not all processes require a full Six Sigma project to reduce the defects. However, all organizations can earn benefits based on the core of Six Sigma:

Reduce the process variations to produce defect-free goods and services.

Tool: Pareto chart

This visual tool shows contrasts between different groups. The Pareto chart illustrates the number of items associated with each group; this sets a comparison of the volumes of each one and allows to identify those with larger size. In improvement cycles, such as Six Sigma, Pareto charts display the effects of the implemented changes.

The Pareto chart highlights the groups with greater impact because of their largest number of elements. This chart can use different details; this enables to analyze different angles; some relevant details are item count, costs, spent time, counting redundant operations and wasted resources.

Vilfredo Pareto was an Italian engineer and economist; he built the following hypothesis: 80% of the wealth is concentrated in 20% of individuals. The Pareto chart seeks to highlight the groups that have the greatest impact; this supports his original theory: most items are related to a few groups.

The Pareto chart uses bars, the height of each bar represents the size of that group. Bars are ordered based on their height, from highest to lowest; this enables to recognize the groups with greater impact and their difference against the smaller ones.

To build a Pareto chart follow the procedure below:

1. Define the relevant groups for the analysis; these groups must be mutually exclusive.

2. Define the proper scale for analysis; it can be based on element count, costs, spent time or any other relevant detail.
3. Define the scope of the analysis. This must clarify which elements are included in the chart.
4. Collect the elements' data, consolidate information and locate them in the proper group.
5. Calculate values for each group and the overall total
6. Draw the area for the graph using 2-axis: horizontal and vertical:

    - Place the groups on the horizontal axis, sort them from larger to smaller minor based on the scale (the scale was defined in step 2).

    - Mark the measurement units of the scale on the left vertical axis (the measurement scale was defined in step 2). The highest point of the vertical axis should cover to the overall total

    - Set a percentage scale in the right vertical axis, from 0 to 100%.

7. Draw bars for each group, the height must match their value on the scale (the scale was defined in step 2).
8. Draw a line to show the consolidated groups' percentage, from left to right.

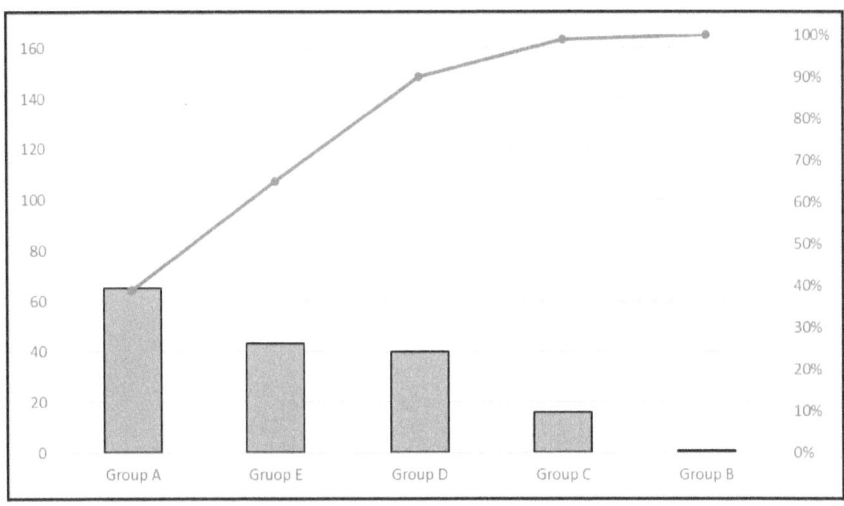

Groups	Items	Consolidated %
Group A	65	39%
Gruop E	43	65%
Group D	40	90%
Group C	16	99%
Group B	1	100%

Pareto chart is a tool that keeps a high similarity to Six Sigma: address issues based on facts. Look at the example below:

Define

A financial services company has identified a problem with its operations. A Pareto chart shows 67% of customers' complaints are related to incomplete services requests; this data belongs to the most recent six months:

Complaint cause	Complaints	Consolidated %
Incomplete service request	150	67.26%
Missing reports and statements	40	85.20%
Expensive fees	25	96.41%
Unrecognized expenses	8	100.00%

Another Pareto chart displays the amounts ($) of operations related to incomplete service requests; the total amount is $3 million. $2.5 million are associated to the incomplete mortgage requests:

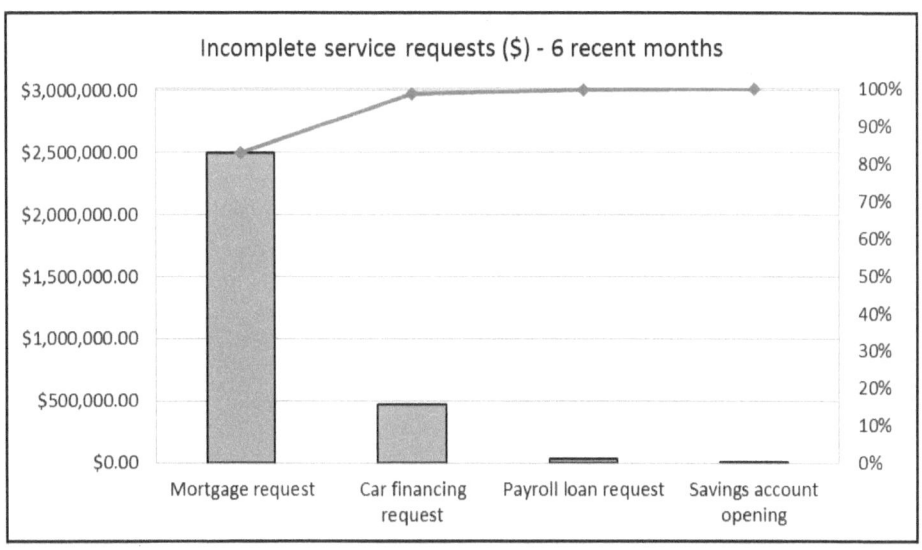

Incomplete service requests	Requests	Amount	Consolidated % (amount)
Mortgage request	40	$2,500,000.00	82.92%
Car financing request	35	$472,500.00	98.59%
Payroll loan request	25	$35,000.00	99.75%
Savings account opening	50	$7,500.00	100.00%

The organization has considered these incidents to develop an improvement project; the goal is to reduce delays in mortgage requests.

Measure

Data from the mortgage loans operations was consolidated. The information belongs to the most recent six operation months.

Following Pareto chart shows amounts ($) for the completed mortgage requests during the last six months. Incomplete requests represent 30% of total mortgages:

Mortgage requests	Request count	Amount	Consolidated % (amount)
Completed	80	$6,000,000.00	71%
Incomplete	40	$2,500,000.00	100%

The Pareto chart below shows the amounts ($) of incomplete mortgage requests. The cases are grouped by delay reason. Missing customer contact data is related to 24 unfinished mortgage requests. The 24 mortgages represent $1.5 million; this is 60% of all incomplete mortgage requests.

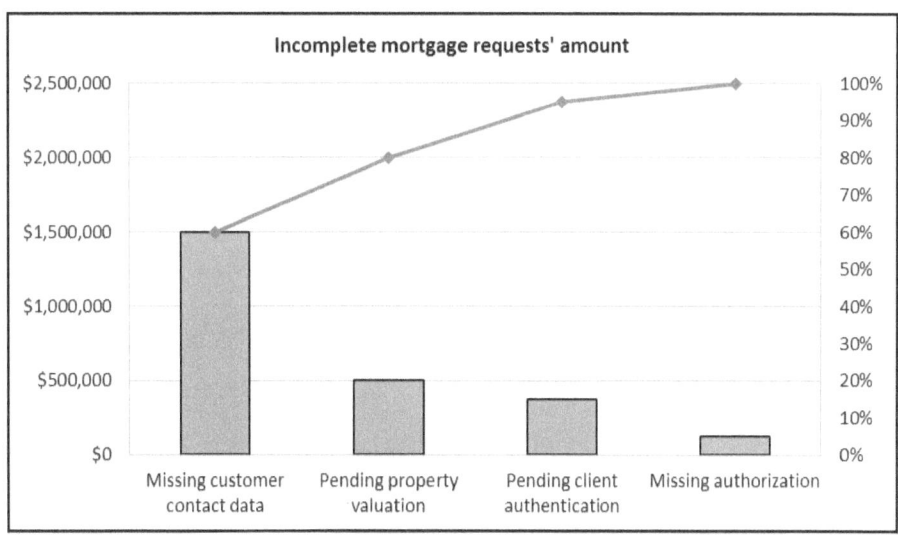

Reason	Requests	Amount	Consolidated % (amount)
Missing customer contact data	24	$1,500,000	60%
Pending property valuation	8	$500,000	80%
Pending client authentication	6	$375,000	95%
Missing authorization	2	$125,000	100%

Analysis

The identified relation between incomplete contact details and 60% of the unfinished mortgage requests, led to consider the mandatory contact details. Two actions were suggested:

1. Reduce the count of mandatory contact details.
2. Accept alternative details such as email and office phone.

The mortgage loans area accepted the proposals.

Improvement

The accepted suggestions were implemented during the following month:

1. The procedure to open mortgage credit was modified; this reduced the count of mandatory contact details and included the alternative contact details.
2. New forms for mortgage procedure have been supplied; these documents match to the new procedure.
3. Previous forms were removed and destroyed to avoid any confusion.
4. Mandatory training sessions were executed, the staff of mortgage loans attended to them.

The details of mortgage operations were consolidated after the implementation of the suggestions; this data considers six months.

The following Pareto chart shows a decrease in the amount ($) of incomplete mortgages requests: from 2.5 million to 1.2 million. This diagram also shows a decrease in the proportion of incomplete mortgage requests: from 30% to 17%.

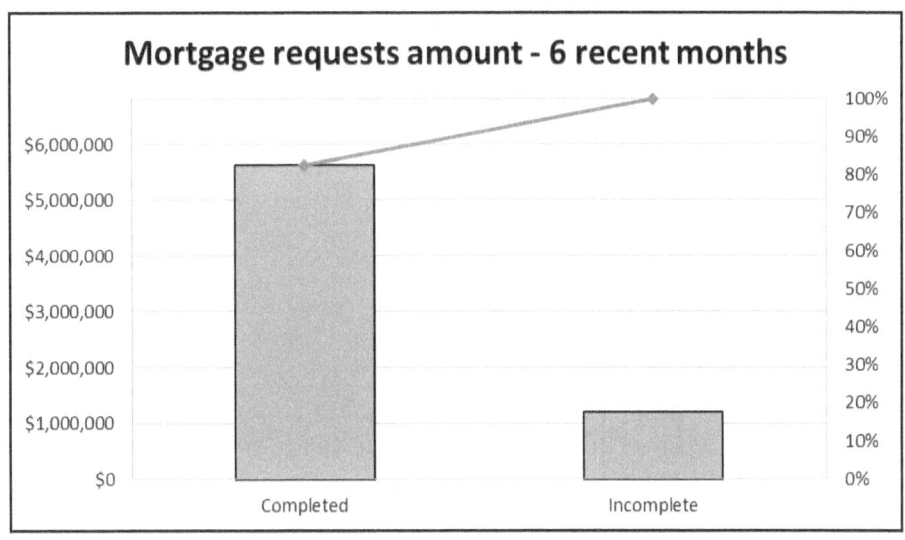

Mortgage requests	Request count	Amount	Consolidated % (amount)
Completed	75	$5,625,000	83%
Incomplete	19	$1,187,500	100%

The following Pareto chart shows unfinished mortgage requests; this also displays for the delay cause. The chart shows that delays caused by incomplete contact details have decreased: from 24 to 3; this also represents a decrease in the amounts ($) from 1.5 million to 0.2 million.

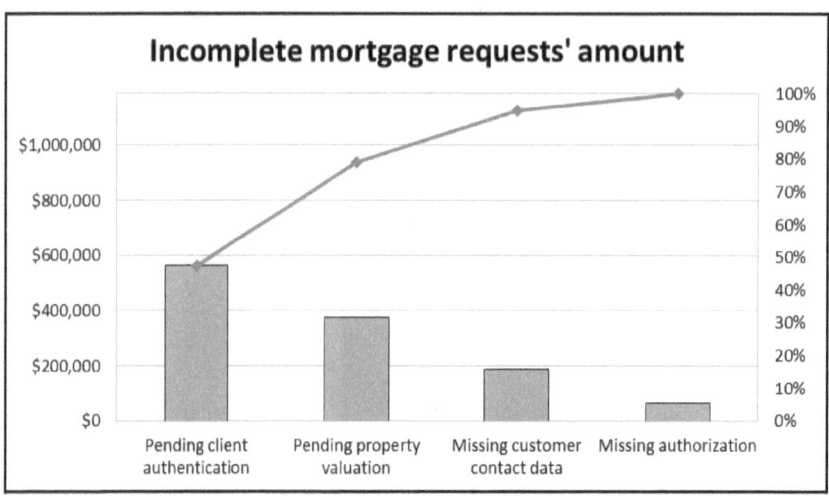

Reason	Requests	Amount	Consolidated % (amount)
Pending client authentication	9	$562,500	47%
Pending property valuation	6	$375,000	79%
Missing customer contact data	3	$187,500	95%
Missing authorization	1	$62,500	100%

The modification in the mortgages procedure seems to generate the desired results.

Control

Additional training will be provided; this is aimed to reaffirm the new mortgages procedure. This action seeks to keep the improvements in the process.

Causes of unfinished mortgage requests will be reported and evaluated every three months. This action will monitor the performance of the process and promptly resolve any unwanted behavior.

In this example the Pareto chart was applied on several moments; these applications were part of the Six Sigma cycle: define, measure, analyze, improve and control.

LEAN MANUFACTURING

Lean Manufacturing is a framework dedicated to the elimination of all kinds of waste; this enables the organization to generate the highest value possible. Lean Manufacturing refers to waste as "muda" and identifies seven classifications:

1. Transportation - Raw materials and products should be transported to the places where are useful. The unnecessary movements generate costs and increases waiting times; the transit exposes resources and products to damages and accidents.
2. Inventory - Stored assets must match with the customers' demand and maintain the execution of operations. Excessive raw materials, unfinished goods and final products represent resources that don't generate benefits; these assets are at risk of lose their value.
3. Movements - The assets of the organization (staff, tools, vehicles) must perform just the needed steps to develop their activities; this represents a practical work. Excessive movements can generate costs, increase work cycles, cause damages and produce injuries.
4. Wait - The raw materials, unfinished goods and final products must be kept moving forward to reach the customers who request them. Bottlenecks, the limits on the operation volumes and the slow pace of the work should be fixed; all this reduces waiting times, the customers will receive products faster and the organization will capitalize its assets faster too.

5. Overproduction - Organizations must produce only the volume of goods and services demanded by customers. Large lots and volumes of operations deliver more products than needed; this produces units which generate no benefit to anyone.

6. Extra processing - The processes and operations must provide the features needed to satisfy the customers. When a product receives unnecessary characteristics, the resources are invested in worthless purposes.

7. Defects - Processes and operations of the organization should produce goods and services aligned to the expectations and free of defects. The presence of errors causes losses and requires additional resources to amend consequences.

Lean Manufacturing is original from Japan, where resources are treasured; this framework seeks to generate higher value from the consumption of resources.

Lean Manufacturing attempts to get rid of every unnecessary element and keep only the ones which generate value. Following actions could be implemented as part of Lean Manufacturing:

- Assess resource consumption at productive activities; then eliminate activities that do not produce enough benefits.
- Implement mechanisms to keep people aware of incidents which need attention, without waiting to be informed.
- Establish restrictions to prevent the generation of errors.
- Stop routine activities that don't generate value and focus on tasks that help the organization and its customers

- Avoid engaging large amounts of resources; keep them available to attend real needs. Keep the supplies within reach of those who use them; this will prevent delays at the operations.
- Keep work environment free from unnecessary items; this maintains fast operations.
- Synchronize the operation times and cycles; this prevents delays and waiting periods.

There are several alternatives to apply Lean Manufacturing; in all of them, the organization should enforce the fair resource investment to generate a higher value.

Tool: Value Stream Map

This visual tool shows the different activities involved in the production of a good or a service. The Value Stream Map provides a complete view of the path traveled by a product; starts at the beginning of its production and reach the delivery to the customer. This tool identifies the consumed resources on the road and the resources invested in creating value; the time is the most common reference to measure the resources volumes.

The development of the Value Stream Map must identify a cycle with two ways:
1. The path of the information, so the organization knows the products to produce and the required resources.
2. The road traveled by resources, unfinished goods and final products; starting with the providers' supply, covering production and reaching the delivery to the customer.

The Value Stream Map highlights some relevant elements using symbols:

Customer/Supplier: External sources provide raw materials or information; these entities exchange goods, services and knowledge with the organization.

Electronic information: this stream uses fast communication channels and enhances coordination

———▶

Manual information: traditional communication channels are applied.

Push arrow: The units move to subsequent production activity, regardless of the demand. Following activities not request supplies, receive it consistently.

· · · · · · · · · ▶

Pull arrow: The units move forward only when customers or subsequent activities request them.

FIFO Connection: Two activities are linked following the First Input First Output order. Units finished by one activity will be processed by the subsequent one, following the same order they arrived.

Shipment: Transportation of raw materials, unfinished goods or final products; these exchanges involve the organization and external entities as customers or providers.

Go see: This symbol marks a point where information is collected by observation to verify the proper performance. Examples: supervisor inspection or inventory review.

Inventory: Storing locations for materials, in unfinished goods and final products.

Kaizen Burst: highlights problems and opportunities for improvement; these points can be modified to reduce waste.

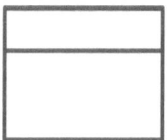

Process: Work established to perform a transformation; this may include methods, procedures, tools and other resources.

Information box: holds additional knowledge regarding specific items of the value stream map.

Kanban Cards: Tickets used to either request the production of units to supply further process or request the replacement of consumed units. These cards help to produce just the demanded items.

Operators: Shows the number of people required to perform certain activities or processes. This symbol helps to identify the involved human resources.

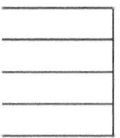

Supermarket: Points where units are available for the ones who need it. Specific activities are responsible for replenishing the taken units. The "supermarket" keeps available just the units consumed regularly in operation; this enables continuous operation.

Material pull: This arrow shows the removal of units from supermarkets; the removed units should be replenished.

Safety Stock: Storage of minimum units; the purpose is to prevent the shortages and disruption of activities. Safety stocks could be temporary.

Databox: This space holds useful details about a specific element of the map. The Databox must be placed close to the referred point and the information enables a better understanding.

Timeline: This thread follows all the stream, it also highlights processing time (dedicated to operations, generating value) and waiting times (consumed by all stream steps).

Value stream map should be based on the actual behavior of the production of goods and services; this requires trustable information and verified facts.

The value stream map includes data on the resources invested in each activity and its use. Following details are included in this tool:

- **Cycle Time:** The time required to complete a specific process that is involved in the production of a good or service.
- **Lead Time:** This time is required to complete the whole production flow; starts with the unit beginning the first task and finishes with the unit ending the last one.
- **Value-added time (VAT):** This time is dedicated to activities that provide value to the product; the results of these activities are relevant for the customers and cause satisfaction.
- **Changeover time:** This is the required time to get the process ready, so it can start to work on a different product. High changeover times delay the production and must be avoided.
- **Uptime:** During this time the productive activities can be performed; this has to consider the incidents that block the work (configuration, maintenance, repairs). The uptime is related to process availability to work.

Value Stream Map provides a common understanding of the path traveled by the products (goods and services) since their creation until reaching the clients; this map helps to develop ideas and execute changes to improve the resource usage. Following factors are relevant for successful Value Stream Maps:

- Use actual data. Recent data, collected from the operations and verified on the field will provide an accurate idea of the behavior; the old data could differ from the current state of the process.
- Single product. The path for each type of goods or services presents particular conditions; it's necessary to focus on a single product to build the accurate map.
- Provide value to the organization. Several symbols and data details could be incorporated into the Value Stream Map; the usage of these elements must be oriented to enrich the communication and develop useful knowledge. The benefit to the organization must drive the usage of many or few symbols and details.

The next example applies the Value Stream Map to a process and presents improvement ideas to reduce waste. This case illustrates the production of a bookshelf in a furniture producer:

QUALITY FOR STARTERS

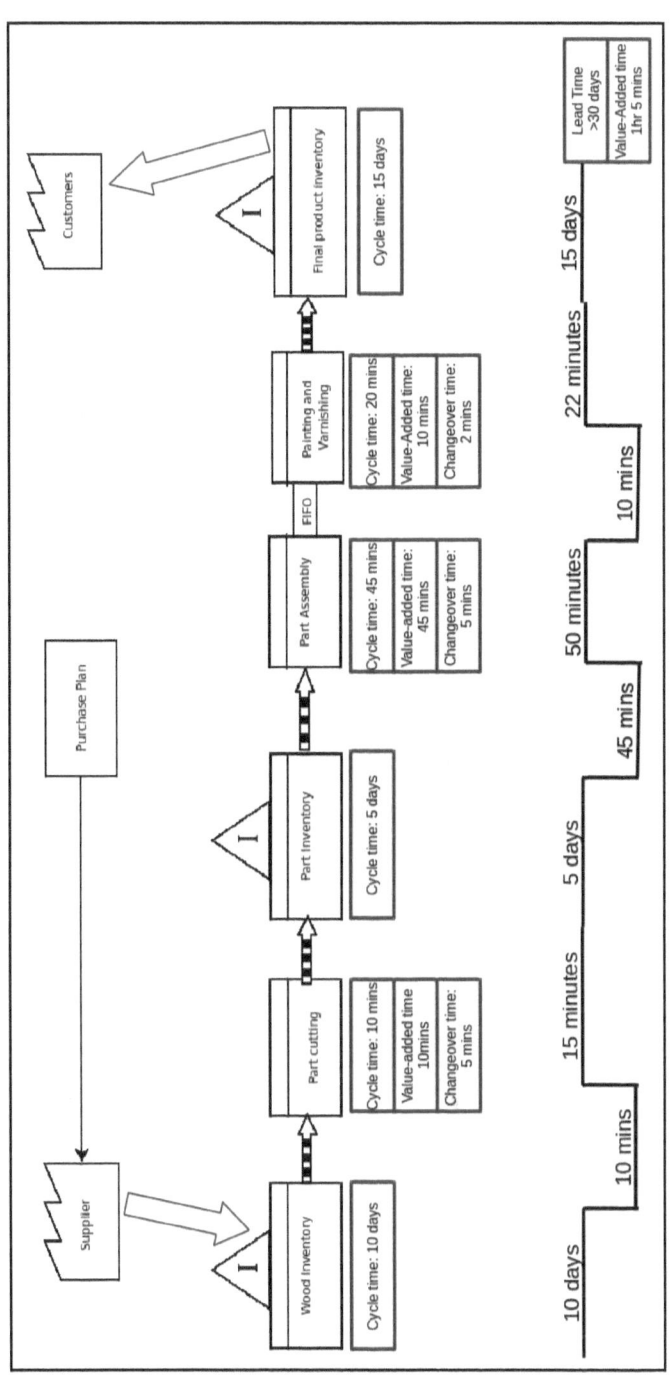

Relevant elements displayed on the map:

- The total lead time is over 30 days, while the total value-added time is 1:05 hours; this shows a high contrast between the time required to produce a bookshelf (about one hour) and the time consumed to take a unit through all the activities (30 days).
- There is no information flow from customers; therefore operations are only based on estimated procurement plan.
- There are three storage stages; these added 30 days to total lead time.
- Changeover times take as much as 5 minutes, this represents a brief wait before starting the production of a new unit.
- Cycle times at non-inventory processes are similar to value-added times; this means the most of their tasks are appraised for customers.

Next map contains the same information; this copy includes improvement ideas in Kaizen Bursts:

QUALITY FOR STARTERS

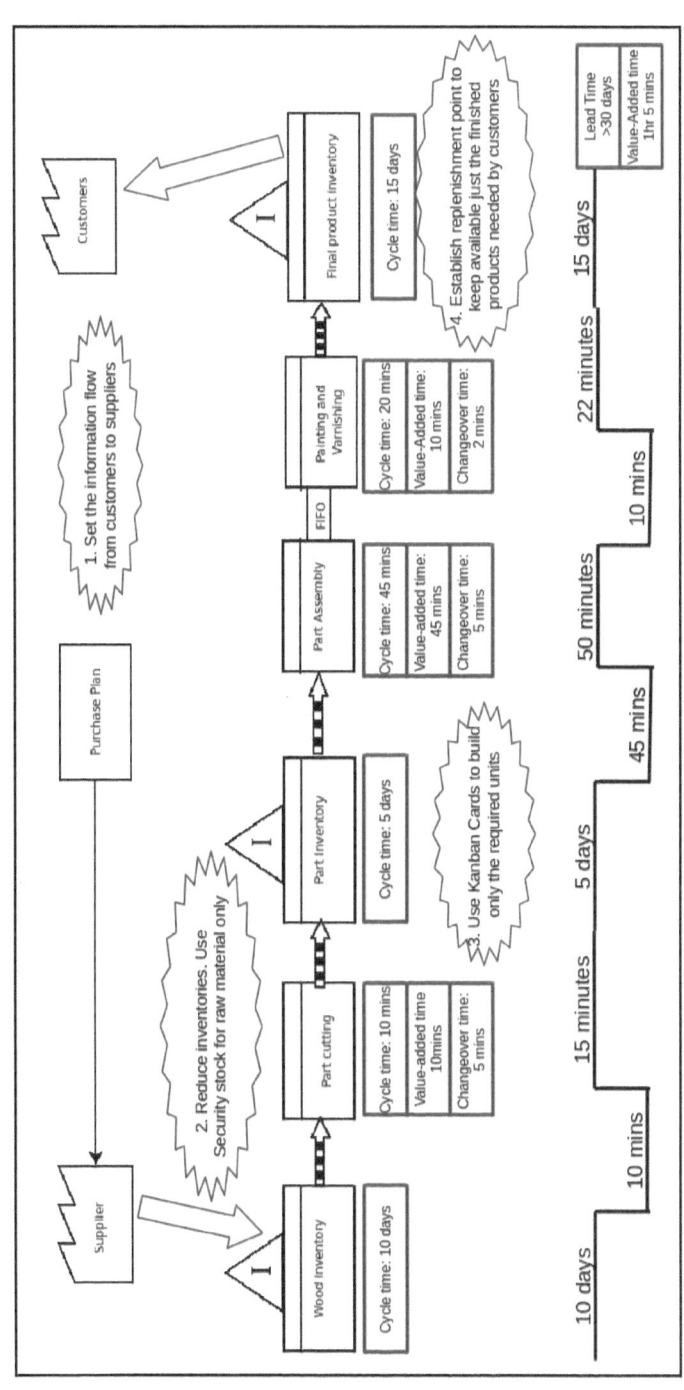

The following Value Stream Map contains a new flow; this introduces the resulting process, after implementing improvement ideas. The improvement ideas are included in information boxes to track the changes:

QUALITY FOR STARTERS

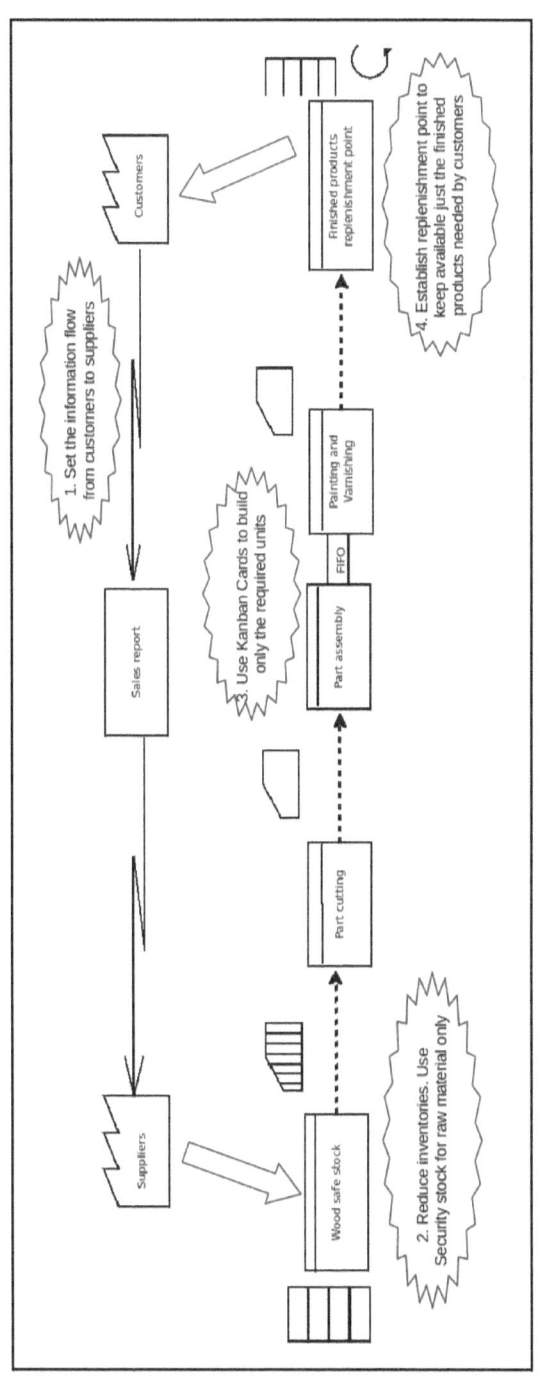

The new Value Stream Map implements the following actions:

1. Set the information flow from customers to suppliers. Base the raw material supply on actual sales.
2. Reduce inventories; this cuts waiting times and engaged resources. Use security stocks for raw material only; these resources can be capitalized faster than manufactured products.
3. Use Kanban Cards to build only the required units. Operations will be based on replenishment.
4. Establish a replenishment point to keep available just the finished products needed by customers.

This example uses the Value Stream Map to enhance resource consumption and reduce waiting times; this executes the Lean Manufacturing ideas.

THE NEXT STEP

All the elements discussed in this book are part of Quality Engineering and contribute to the success of organizations. The purpose of quality is clear: generate benefits by delivering goods and services capable of satisfying expectations and requirements.

The content of this book is intended to help in quality implementation:

- The four elements establish the basis of quality in organizations.
- The seven tools allow performing simple activities to implement the quality.
- The three frameworks expand the perspective about actions to refine the quality in organizations

There are several alternatives, concepts and tools that are useful in the development of quality. However, there is no universal and fail-safe solution. It is necessary to be clear about the purpose of the quality, considering the reality and the context faced by the organization; this helps to develop proper actions and achieve the best results.

I wish you get the greatest success in this field. For quality reasons I am open to receive feedback that helps me to improve this content; I'll be happy to receive your comments and suggestions at the following address: lenriquediazh@gmail.com.

www.ingramcontent.com/pod-product-compliance
Lightning Source LLC
Chambersburg PA
CBHW030443220526
45464CB00006B/2398